Is-nes

To Brian,
The Truest Friend
and first soldier in the
Fight.

HOORAY,
wherever you SHALL stray.

Michael

9-26-97

Is-ness: Selected Poems

Michael Hanahen

VANTAGE PRESS
New York

FIRST EDITION

Published by Vantage Press, Inc.
516 West 34th Street, New York, New York 10001

Manufactured in the United States of America
ISBN: 0-533-12174-4

Library of Congress Catalog Card No.: 96-90828

0 9 8 7 6 5 4 3 2 1

Contents

Preface

My poetry serves to alert, alarm, incite, and inspire.
It carries within its self-constructed fog
The ideal of questions, the telling of a rambling journey
(A holy salute to vision).

With meaning unknown to the wisest bard,
I do not toil in that arena, nor do I wish
To pretend myself a leader, of anything—
Creating herds is no objective of mine.

The horrible stink of grammar, the shrill
Of anarchism, the seemingly lacking
Connective tissue, will no doubt serve to sicken
The high members of the dream-art network.
But my poetry was never intended to please them.
I'm like the gnat behind your ear, buzzing.

Hymn or curse, it is the individual reader's responsibility
to
Leave with it, or simply leave it.

Is-ness: Selected Poems

Praise Ye

Praise ye
who tend to assault the senses.
Praise thee
who lives to leap the mortal fences.
Praise he
who creates to destroy the cages of the consensus.

It's all here and waiting
as we are all now and happening.
The ancient word is sounding.

Give us back our right to religious theater
or remember the murder.

10/14/97
* Religious in the broad sense. Freedom of expression and thought more literally. Directed at the establishment (obviously Christians) who have condemned the murderers for their resistance to the message of the messiah, while now resisting w/ persistence.

Eve of Innocence

My friends and I
gathered to strand ourselves
in a low-rent urban outpost
on the other side of our conscience.

'Twas the icy winter of rebellion

American under godless greed
with poor blood and beggars' hearts.
Days of Jeopardy laughed at,
experiments implemented,
ordainment risked.

We swapped stories,
luckless Fables, The Modern Blues.
With regional slur of things seen and had
through lies and knowledge.

Tenement hustle—whiskey runs
No time to think or work
while on the Eve of innocence.

We got drunk and danced with strange night women,
plunged our seed into the city.
Discovered the moon through other eyes.

→ Stepping into another place
w/in ourselves as a means of
temporary escape. Ultimately & inevitably
going back to occupy the life we
have decided to live.

Floodings

We will live ourselves out in the space of time or years.
We will live ourselves out in a flood of mass hysterical life.

As thought floods the streams of humanity,
And makes weak the truth of description.

Free thought abrogates an objective + absolute truth.

As love floods ego limited to
The anatomy of physical perfection.

Love is blind

We don't know truth. Truth is beyond us. There is one truth, but it is beyond our capacity.

As birds flood rooftops and skylines, now awed
In companies of mechanical strangers,
To whom flight is further work of genius.

As drugs flood each street disowned,
Giving America weird unities,
Bound in lone whole distortions.

As cars flood highways and interstates
Rides through reality, pathways
In which everywhere is reachable, except
The smooth forests of our remembrance.

As sex floods teenage acrobats, out to perform,
While Sunday school teachers weep immorality's tear.

As hearts flood arms to hold or make certain,
Legitimizing the self.

As distance floods earth and eternity,
Man vs. Father vs. money.

The dilemma is to understand, many are lost and don't want to understand.

Diseased or dying o'er unkept consciousness.
As space floods the mind left to stray
Empty corridors where a real universe unwinds
    perception,
Nothing known but rivers and voids.

As death floods change, giving chance and wonder
Movement and new beginnings
To the old life phase.

As we are a vast breath
Flooding existence.

very true -

- we seem to be OR are insignificant, while being intricate, complicated and sophisticated.

Tape Jazz

Women of work and hunger
Thunder an' wet bride excitement—go away.
Let me Flash on silence
'Til Tomorrow's Time hurries in
On winged misery,
Washing the gutter's snuff up to my door.

There is a certain self found in solitude.
While Tape Jazz runs clear consciousness
In the background
        (O Sensual City)
The urban mistress, quite a Beautiful wreck,
Dances, stoned on alternative editions
Of liberal growth.
Wallowing in deviant Freedom
Daring entrance—screaming sadness.
But she'd bring certain unnamable horrors in with her.
Proudly wearing her urban thorns
An' singing rock-n-roll genius junk.

A certain other reveals itself thru' loneliness!
Time is night, rolling over, undressing itself for me.
Oh and I'm sniffing nature's white lily heaven.
For my earth is a garden,
Of grooves, of glimpses into idiot gods
Confessing their stubborn insistence
On paralyzed sloth.

Being alone is petrified divinity.
I've laid an army of words down for
Old loves.
Now I curse their well-to-do's

An' Lord save you's—for I have remained
Whole as any-one
        saint or whore.

So tonight I lie worldly naked,
Heart beating illuminated oneness.
While Tape Jazz runs clear consciousness
In the background.

Some Mutt

Some mutt in a backyard barking as if the moon
Was just some white-lined intruder.
What presence to believe he is the only guardian
Of land and life.
Do wings flap within his chest
As well as ours?
If history's ditch is not waiting
At the end of this time.

What must he make of all these streets and chiefs
Who have legislated his wild?
Does he curse Karma for a dog's life,
Mad at this merry-go-round existence.
Or does he thank some mysterious animal lord.
For the sake of being instead of having to become!

Does he roam with the least of wonder,
Or think us odd in our hurry.
And for what is the hurry, would he conclude—
As I have.

Fly Off

Fly off, crazy bird
Be our beacon symbol
Our inflamed desire
There are greater heights and gifted treasures.
No boundaries to hold the wanton.

Whiskey and mystics,
Tools of a working earth.
To incite our senses five
To inspire each nerve burning within a hushed reality.

The poor of meat and wine
Of avenues and drunks and Indian brothels
Blurred visions, raw prophecies
You who are left gnawing on that bony
White marrow of life.

Run way far
Seek yourselves out
Call on wisdom, democracy
Every form of witchcraft and splendor
Each evening, all madness,
Go chasing down the farthest falling star
Guided on by sleep dreams an' rainbow myths
We shall have our eyes to glimpse
The immaculate!

Union shall be our task
With every emphasis on passing into one.
Diverging forms—reflective images
We'll build the bridge between
Body and soul.

We'll be of dance, liberty and love.
Created as prayers from a flesh.
And art given from eternity.

Then finally we'll come to rest divine
As beasts can be.

is this the one?

Fires of a Youth

We were beasts on a shore
where the sun was never to set.
Wild whores who dreamed orgies of the mind
geniuses all, who through windows of a soul
saw our kingdom well.

We were damned without purpose
or construction of worth
and so lived the holy life.
We the brave Fools
were the weavers of Fantasy
whose bride was the nakedness of night.

O Father O Mother
O large industries of man, so knowing
we've wilted into your arms
now with dry lips an' sagging breasts
shall to breed, contempt.

While a languid candle is lit in the distance
for the bastard child to stray towards

with runnin' hope for the eternal bloom.

The National Science

Priests, Poets, Philosophers, Parents
Artists all, and all are thieves.
Thieves of beauty and of time itself.
Here to sing like ancient sailors of a sister faith.

To abound with cosmic energy
Wielding the national science.
To master the dark hours of immortality
Bringing justice to heaven and hell alike
To chant in free chorus of lands and lakes,
Skies and fields—hearts and hope.

To merrily behold the stars' grand drama
An' simply accept insanity of existence.
To empower words an' wisdom.
An' light each century that lies 'neath
The maker of all images.

Humanity

As the willow to the wind will bend
As the creeks for the storm must rise.
Like heavy rains driving hard against the night.
We're bound to race the river's current,
Unbeatable as sundown.
So we'll be here to wonder, study
          and regret.

And the sea-life will live on
In an underwater world.
As our wilderness is to remain
As the wisest old architecture.
While space, first home of mind and matter
Shall hover eternally as the dream of our unknowing.
So we'll be here to breathe, behold
          and pity.

And the streets will run longer
As cities grow out still farther.
While eyes glare out of the crowd's unknown
Configuration.
Each entity forever feeling set apart.
Not by mere costume or clothing
But rather a soul divine as undying
So we'll be here to sacrifice, glorify
          and weep.

And stars will peak out
As for uncountable years they have
And the sun will burn down
On a brilliant bouquet of farms and gardens.
While within solitary shadows we're to find

A stalking silhouette, a shapeless grace
Playfully elusive as ever any reason could be.
'Til finally the seasonal chants are heard
From the homeland
So we shall be here to witness, rage
and multiply.

From a Crossroad

I

O misty eve of remembrance
O dreams of a flowing faith in tomorrow.
I've been to the dirty swamps
where stagnant waters lie,
and aching hearts bleed-concentrated in misery.
I've wandered far o'erlooking
lordly seas—heard the rush of waves
eternal, pushed onward by winds
of a wondrous breath.

A scene of journeys at a willful crossroads.
Dusty paths of memories,
Yesterdays compared to the vision (progress).

Beat loners, bruised an' dragging
ragged limbs across the year.
Lazy stoners—sickly cross-eyed farts
carrying high delusions of grandeur, an'
ill-gotten gains from minds wrecked
to know—arrive at their crossroad
pleading indifference, 'neath fat, cold
moons of universe.

II

Desert's child, born to solitude
and their own nightmare, immaculate,
conceived in dim rooms, where a candle's
flame feeds the fear of thought.
To be growing holy, or simply
growing, 'til gone.

A mass of weary servants to the
grizzly grind of daily suppression
for which we cannot find fault,
for who here is serious enough to cast
that historical stone upon themselves?
Mad galloping horseman showered in
ancient western confetti (cowboy heroes forever),
outlawed in their freedom with silver
bullet guns to win their way.
All have come to thee, crossroad,
begging change of purpose.

Star-spangled patriots
saluting government, all ways
so noble, so undying in their steel-fisted
grip on the morals of loyalty.

III

Negroes of the Jungle
tribes of urban warfare
aborigines of loping highways
syndicates of greed,
now stagger through wastelands, miles long
To reach their fork-eyed crossroads.

O Time, where nothing
pervades o'er you, like insane
armies in roaming.
Oh, to the rambling hours that leave you
twisting—all vague and circling
yourself.
The choices, the chances,
the fixed frenzy of suffering decisions.
Right or wrong—best or worst,
Where, in the clearing, crossroads serve
To prove the human rider's destiny unclear.
Trying all ways to catch the lone
miracle in running.

The Ugly Nest

The ugly nest
    infested brew
under the city
    where spirits stir.

Semblance of Reality
    tender night promise.

Karma players peeling away natural man.

Madness cries, "The womb is dry."
Dust in the throat, a collar around the neck.

I'm no driver, no rider, I'm no thing
But life seething at the surface
Hollow 'neath the weight that carries
timelessness into being.

Slumbering I breathe, worshiping
The oulaw star, my great ancestor's forest,
And the mansion that holds my bride of grace,
The season of awakened silence.

Neon Atmosphere

Neon atmosphere
Cloud bursts in the atomic twilight.
Evening scriptures in the pale moonlight.
Shadows house the holy and the haunted.
The weary and wise—screaming angels.
Is this it?
What about salvation, what about damnation?

I died for the hell of this war,
because they said death was lunch for the
meat eaters that glimmer and fade.
Would we be forgiven our beliefs
if we believed in forgiveness?
Where did the dust of the soul drift?

Oh, Body Ravaged

O body, ravaged in flashing mirrors,
raped by innate crisis.
Kneeling at the gateway of woman
I plead entrance
without question or cause.
I, arriving for the softly woven touch
that inflames in me
a thousand hells of eternity.

O body, where hardened beggars come to lie
as roving gamblers make their appeal on you.

Bony muscle—surging nerves
that tempt to dare—flesh destructive
tendencies when left to lone evenin' slumber.
Belly full of guts and ash,
throats heaving curses of blood.
Every second a movement of miracle and existence,
and all in the act of sensation,
and all in the name of desire
(revolving in mortal orbits).

Rusty Palaces

Oh, hear the rusty palaces now shaking.
The wobbly towers in their breaking
will bring new ruins.
But a child's faith could remake anew
all his elders daily undo.

Oh, see the gutters running blood
into our garden.
Yes, the dream in dying may be pardoned,
if the peaceful ease of sleep
would find us a soul wallowing in the deep.

Oh, feel the mighty act of life, idealized
beyond one and imagined.
As the space of many, if realized,
may be too much to bear.
O vast universe whirling in me
  out there!

Forest Echoes

'Neath skies that hang an azure image
shall I take these steps
into a forest visage,
and in chorus will I hear
the majestic birds' natural hymn
as in times long ago
the same was sung by Indians.

And low the clouds will I pass
on way to rivers runnin'.
And through paths winding, a gentle breeze shall guide
'til I come to lie on sandbanks
in an afternoon of sunnin'.
And I shall dream of gypsy caravans
that might once have passed this way,
o'erriding the silence
that does endure most hours of the day.

Amid the meadow, sun and noble standing trees
will I at last glimpse upon mortal worthiness.
In shade of branches or mid-day brightness
I'll know the life of this living wilderness.

O sky, stars and universe, I call to thee
who are of a different birth.
I have seen your gods of grandeur.
They have alerted me to the long suffering of this earth.
But I have only to ask,
Let these mere beauties exist long after I have gone,
and autumn's last leaf has fallen.
For like seasons in their turning
in all ways we shall live on.

Woman

There is a profoundness in the way
she leans, just right, against the gnarled tree.
More mystic than the climax
of our thought could ever yield,
you who leave men jealous
of even your shadow.

Do you go marching nude
into the summer waves?
Would you be the sea's only lover?
Do you leap for blistering suns
or lie shinin' by the moon's sad light?
Did I hear the crickets singing odes
to you in your evenin'?
Has the meadow's fairest rose only
been imitating your beauty?

For the merchants are buying up
Turquoise to rest by your side,
as contented beggars have gathered
together sea shells to place
at your feet.

But your dreams, I wager, are
waiting to mate with one who sees
past vanity's flesh, beyond
Today's mortality,
and into your vast space of
silences and freedoms
deep to alone.

Mortality

Vision of the lamb
Sweet little lamb musing in the cornfield,
White like Siberia
Sad as nature,
Shotgun blast from behind camouflage mask.

Suburban rabbit, aged and tamed
Evening creeping through the freshly cut grass—
Killed for good luck—yup, ya betcha'
And luck's a funny thing!

A tired troop sagging in the green vine forest,
The general grunt himself is crying,
"We shall fight forevermore!"

While the mama lion waits in the bush
For midnight's secret feeding,
Milky death on the warring highways.

Mortality takes all comers,
Makes them loud and proud to live;
Then spits them out into the void.

Sexual Bloom

I imagine
Every lover you've ever had
Has called you his best.
I'm sure it's true.
True indeed, for I too have stood
In the pleasant glow of your nakedness.
I too have seen a bloody rose
Bloom from the sheets.

Strange—all parts of your anatomy named and labeled
In letters or as memories
Of lust's bright abandonment.

Your ego massaged by the hungry hands
Of meat eaters.
Your heart pricked by the thorns of vanity.
Deranged beauty
So overexposed and neutral.

Come ye who seek thy one-night true love
To build future fantasies upon.
Also come ye of the sloppy kiss
And the sweaty want—it's the ancient madonna myth.

See the angel nymph in the starry night
The mistress dancer ode to luxury
Bound to sin
(Have you enslaved others with your desire
Or has your desire enslaved you to them).

For I am a born-again virgin
To this world of body
To the erection of touch
To the penetration of treasures.
True. Noble. Sacrificed.
Now I will draw you a map to my sex.
Down the dark caverns of aloneness
Along the temples of guilt
Within the rivers of surging nerves/temptation's flight.

But beware of the wolves, they are unfed.
Also beware of the rains of remembrance.
Most unholy and hard falling.
And if you happen to make it through,
I shall see you in love.

Bleeding Chance Revival

Bleeding chance revival
    Give me the favor of love.
I'm a northern brat,
    More than that I'm America's creation.

Holy moans from the river banks.
    I'm the spark of rage.
Forgetting karma in my footsteps.
    Forgoing each blue angel that persists
Upon my shoulder.
    No queen will soon undress for me,
As no death will come to grant me
    Greatness in my absence.

It's each second that ruins me.
    The past like a bright ghost once haunted
With ill-timed attacks.
    But I soon learned to pervert it,
And it has now become unquestionable
    In its slender recollections.

And the future though once was drunk deep
    Within the bones, seemingly to prove fear,
Has now become my servant of forgiveness.
    But it's each second that holds reality up as relative,
And terrifies each moment's slippery chance.

Deep wanton posturing
    I glide willful through each secondary response.
(Who is that) in the corner flashing naked exposure.
    I'm unwanted in this peace that the liberal seeks.

Words are ripe though mere echoes.
    Dreams the sad forms of deliverance.
And I'm each day a new kind of mystery,
    A clothed statue of consequence,
And unsheltered experience
    With Gods and geeks fondling the heart.
Letting it ride.

O Hail Beauty

Oh, hail beauty
Let me find its glimpse,
its chance toward liberty,
its declaration of glory.
Its face like dreams seething abandonment.

To love thee,
respecting of life,
to chant or dance,
the psalm sung for freedoms
    of sky or ground
    of kiss or tear
and the sky of our masses,
O maker of angels, unknown.

Bring your victims to sleep
where they will be shown the phantasms
of inner miracle magic
as the scheme of meaning unfolds.

American Bones

There are no original pick-up lines anymore!
Men demented in cosmic toil, longing for beauty,
But where hast thou flown since the liberating war of
 rights?
Old ragged, yellow teeth, hangnail beauty
Lost in the struggling dawn.
The butcher's wife—she knows where the meat hangs.

Bodies clash in the being of ecstasy,
And what of this body—the body as prison?
Fantasies of freedom lapping in orbit,
Yet now clothed in mortal whimpering,
Hung up on the alibis of fashion,
The liberating virtues as named our birth and death,
Sex being the ego of both.

Young lad lost in the lonesome dream of wet ecstasy,
 turned nightmare
Old maiden, pale faced, dressed in evening's hood,
Shackled to everything she fears, which is
Everything she doesn't know, or
Everything she's afraid to know.
American bones rattling in the wilderness town.

We're all marking time, trying to die
'Till we inevitably get it right,
Longing to penetrate the sea's wet dream
In the vast African night.

The Great Night Charmer

Silence, the great night charmer.
We're the Kerouac myth,
The alienated swing shift
The outsider, sacred an' scared in knowing
Of the dark loom that hangs o'er
This vast ghost city.

I say, "Is Transcendental Jazz still breathing?"
Miles Davis, dead long.
Leadbelly and Bessie are archives
In some internalized museum.
Yet the rhythm and chanting
Still abound
In soulful summer houses,
Or in autumn's brown eye, tearing
'Neath moons of freedom.

But grand New York is big,
infested. Let's zoom through the wet-
paved streets, outward to the highways
of abandon an' dreams
across desolate prairies
through cotton blossoms, around mountains,
into meadows up high altitudes,
down canyons endless miles long—
Where a strong history still remains
Visions of a land by dusk
An' the sweeping stars of night fall.
Time rolling outward in all ways.

With mystical virgins
laughing drunk.
Long past the midnight hour.

Self-love Bows

Self-love bows back into infancy.
On the sands of fatal contemplation,
I wade back to stylized notions.
Innocent posturing.
Dreaming blue insecurity
Now made real through mirrors and crowds.
Absence of identity.
Self-love reels in the vast life pool.

Soulful leper, exiled.
God dollar worship
Bahama Indian genocide.

An' that self-love we groan to grasp
Is but a sequel to youth's bright-eyed swagger,
Extending across a million
Moons of cosmic folk.
Swollen history, indeed.

A Streaking Shadow

A dead boy on the side of a Denver highway,
A streaking shadow submits no cause only conquest.

A circling bird soars overhead
Mad engines roar down designated routes

And the deep sky tells nothing
But turns a twilight blue
Letting night in for keeping.

Worlds revolve!

Fast Glory

Like a Ferlinghetti tramp
Like Rimbaud's ghost haunting still;
My tribe saw Buddha raging
And hit the void running.

Let that moon come shining
Lighting the landscape,
Insighting the eye of the invisible, the untamed.

Let the sea roll worldly
Over the rocks and into our thought
Knowing the unknowable is unthinkable.

Let the city reflect its earthly light.
I'm a neon magnet, prowling past
The culture's serpents, a nation's energy.

Grab that fast glory,
Named fame, fantasy, easy soul enlightenment
And quick death.

The Jaws of Time

Shall I not escape
The jaws of time that bite.
The hands that grip my fate,
That infinitely has bound me to which I write.

I now see our plague lingering in the distance,
And my senses finally achieve what the dead
Have long since known.
My vision adheres to earthly battles yet begun.
My tongue spits fire from the depths of the void.
My flesh happens upon broken glass that scars belief
Like youth's image unknowingly raped on the midnight
altar.

We must rally around unions of ideas
Or I will be forced to write for the dead only.
We must overthrow this false reality of
Equal injustice.

For our libraries of thought have chased
Us into conformed consciousness,
And God will not soon forget our artful suicide,
Nor the many laws to police the mind,
Nor the moral mention that was never made,
Nor the great ancient architecture we left behind.

Breathing Prophecy

Prophecy returns us to brief writhing wars
And plain hope of insect survival.

Island ocean jewel

Dry meat carcass

Neon circus freeways

She in the crackling mist of dawn
Awoke furious crimes of passion.
Hopeless queen
Eyes like kingdoms.
Let me back inside the gates of your ruins.

Seeing all movements in oneself at once.

We search over and over again
For the big sinking dream.
Fenced in
Where abandonment first began.

Languid summer.

Wild Flower

Bloom, heavenly wild flower on the meadow,
sprout your colors, mystic, in the rain.
Hatch those petals, fleeting, oh beautiful life.

Grow wise an' be gone swift
as the pleasant seasons shift.

Warming self in sun
upon lazy pastures of resting.
Turning to the cool shades of evening
letting any open eye glimpse the immaculate.

Seen in the rosy buds of your solitude—
easy to exist.

Journey—Full

Eyeball to the windowpane
static radio tempts indifference
(for these eyes are a kind of tired
no prophet could endure.
I'm breathing sentiments of thy-self,
wondering what radiant identity shall come
to carry me away.

Now with lonely visions
in the blue afternoon,
I'm chasing fate, straying downtown.
Book stores and Kamikaze Fortune Tellers,
    calico mannequins peering from store fronts.
    original liberty music players
    desolate beside money jars,
    orphaned from pop modern bars
    new blooded mystics in old crack houses
    the well endowed and wifeless
    buying nakedness, selling futures.

Oh, the poor void shines bright
in each indescribable eye of the desperate.
Gypsies of city/Frontier gangs
what beauty had you in a tender youth.
What wet revolutions were dreamt in beds
of safety and soft promise.

O weary rage/O timeless haze
delivered to abandon.
Icy space of rejected gods,
begging for purpose.

I'm walking into eternity
one step at a time.
With optimism sagging.
For America has failed to reduce its prejudice
towards the truth.

Leaving me struggling to remain
the fat greasy patriot
of street reality, dark ecstasy.

Existing to exit,
yet not escape!

Silver Sea, Lap Your Ancient Wonder

Silver sea, lap your ancient wonder
your blue eternity of wet lords and
deep sunken lands.

Hunter shark—breaking the surface
with a Fin of Primitive Fear,
let me see your marble darkened eyes.
Roll over,
the white-fanged Frenzy
of your giant Life.

Hold me 'neath your current,
wrap me in your wise old
underworld.

A Kind of Blindness

Through windows on windstorms
Puddles glazed as mirrors
Eyes a distant inch off
That I'm fast to flee
Upon the stirring of sight.

And yet, I'm forever looking, gazing, glimpsing or facing
The lazy grins of women at sundown.
Wandering the beaches with straight spine
And windy hair.
Always sneaking quick peeks
At squinty-eyed hustlers
Bowed in shadowy doorways,
Lone and discontent with positions unreached—
Grizzly goons of a clenched fist and hidden tear.

I could long to live with ears that hear
The sure-running streams of fate.
I mean really live to touch the bleached
Skin of an attractive get.
I mean to say I would knowingly taste
The worm-rotting apples of lost orchards
Or forsaken groves,

If only all Indian marble eyes were to spin inward,
As the blue sea eyes went blind in depth,
And the hazy autumn brown eyes would lose mere vision
Down dark halls of travel.

So stumble, sick mule or man
Up unsteady mountains.
With no more sight than the bat,
Who bound to his cave,
Has learned innate response.

Like rainbows of intuition,
Like dreams of guidance or intrigue.

The lovers of night and skin deep
Soul knowers, are sure to see
Lucid, beyond day or finally setting dusk.

Magic or Misery

There was an inquiry into magic or misery.
The Troubadour was a ghost,
Ode to the answer of his envy.
The Flag-staff was petitioned to praise
The warden of their souls.
Who himself was only a grunt
To the empress of his enchantment.

Windy horizons
Of dawn's day breaking
All too soon to be descending into dusk
Formed to Fall or Flee
Reckoned like every other
In nature's wrapped anarchy.

Oh, play on, in the deep midnight, starry bright
In the flower beds of your youth or sleep
In the deathless TV screens of our heroes
In the bodies being, clothed an' vague
In your dearest Friend's most Familiar pose
In your world rocked to witness
The war guns of ambition's giants.

And through to your cozy garden trip
Upon your ancient escaping ship.
Where one does seek to see
The kingdom of Magic or Misery.

I'm Gazing Heavy

I'm gazing heavy into the morning.
The street lights are of a yellow glow
Hung on wooden poles that surge electric fire.
A bent tree like some primeval past forgotten
Mingles with the wind.

Next door's furnace hums a gentle nuisance.
The sleeping sounds of a world's people
Mixes with nature's peace blowing directionless.

What savage maiden here sat in yesterday's time,
And looked upon the same waking sky,
Letting her toes rest in the dew-soaked grass,
Or leaned to approach the day yet arriving
With thoughts that strayed, arresting hope.

My god sighing a windy hymn
In the magnificent dark turning dawn,
In my solitary stance within the universal,
In these wide eyes that glimpse general beauty.

Sanctuary

The angel of innocence
Pays respect to my midnight mood,
And weak-whined suffering,
Cursed with ugly fingers
That weave magic.

I caress holy sleep with images of death
And the thought of it being named tragic.
These realms that I run from
Are the deepest memories I cling to.

And so, like the Indians who
Made the forests their temple
With dance and tribal worship,
I seek shelter with the searchers
Forgotten on the highway.

Manhood suffers on my back,
While childhood stays tied to my hip.
Help!
The flurry of invisible crossroads.
The view of the naked.
Passage of power.

Warm Garden Slumber

Warm garden slumber
Lapse of anarchy.
What is this film running fluid doubt,
these wars for luxuriant emblems to fill
the void with illusionary faith?

The knife of deception twisted into the church.
Dedicate yourself to the degree,
to evening TV, to crowds of cunts an' cocks,
born to suffer in mirage after mirage,
drowning in majestic disguise.

We're the blood and guts of schoolyard laughter.
The bad guys wearing bandanas.
We're the poets who own not their words.
We're America dying angelic deaths.

Lone Rider

Lone rider
cloaked in darkness
for the hoax of a road's purpose.

Lest you run never far
an' still go blind in the beauty
of the most lost of horizons.

  Wilderness of orchards
  freedom down valleys.

Beat traveler
honed for the highway
an' its dutiful wisdom.

Though anarchy can be as still
as the ice cliffs that hang in amazement,
in the minds of our drifting.

  Ancient tree wonder
  sad flowing rivers.

To Walk Concrete Paths

'Till our suffering Flesh Fades, decays
Or moves mysterious into some outer musical like limit.

We here are left to walk concrete paths
In shadows of a silk moon.
Where devils groan indignant to our softer side
That may in times of quiet crisis
Whisper lullabies.

What scream heard far yonder
From brothers, mates, or strangers,
Prove these hours a wretched test
For you to care, full open
To the world's curse of chaos?

So can you with faith iron firm
Not mute the beauty
That seeks to destroy you
Like a madman's love.

Poor Boy Rebel Blues

The kid just didn't want to go to college.
Felt there were other experiences to acknowledge.
He wanted to hustle and jive—sing and dance,
Roam around, get lost, get found,
Get out of town,
Go on the road.

The kid just wouldn't be a player,
Institutionalized for life, which seems the modern prayer.
But the Army, Navy, Air Force, Marines
Didn't exactly sound like a viable out either,
Head shaved, named, numbered, uniformed;
It just wasn't his thing.

And when the issue of money arose,
And Mama and Papa kneeled at their pew for the last time
To save a demonic soul.
He thought he'd go runnin' guns to peasant third world
communities
Or deal 'em stateside to the bad ass gangs,
Or easier still, he could start smuggling grass
Across the border.
Weekend rides on down to Mexico,
Loose rolling senoritas, lost angel tramps,
Drunken come-ons in cantinas.

The kid just wouldn't go to school,
Felt it was a bunch of bull shit.
All those fees for that never perfected wisdom
Of an academic's degree.
Getting blessed by the gods of a buck.
Gonna' miss that sixty thousand dollar car though,
And the women that come with it, upon payment.

Now where he wanders today
Nobody can really say.
It's said he's been through your town,
In your city, here and there, all around,
Never notably fitting in.
I myself heard he was out there, somewhere
In the wastelands of youth's rebellion.

Fervor

Governmental mind from birth enslaves
Animals like us
The mass of graves.
Atomic human energy
Lethergy, leprosy
Mortality's fence
A thinker's consequence
Old souls solutions
In bars of dissolution.
A love of love,
Ignoring self.
A need to want
Adorning wealth.
Ocean miles of shit,
Ozone holes in the sky.
Any god still unseeable
To wanton eye.
Naked
Born
Sex of bones
'till sweating death groans
Shall leave sun or snow.
Rain winds,
Ancient canyons
Within we go
To tempt or dare
Life, all the way.

The Moon's Fool

What is he—some kind of freak?
Dangling from a ledge
Perched on the edge of madness (wisdom)
Climbing the walls of a skull
And risking the loss of his blood.

Is he really better off
Being an old dog in his cups?
Would some job, church, woman, reason,
Place or dignity,
Wrestle him away from always
Wanting to go d
o
w
n

Digging into the neon
Like a moon's fool does?

The years have been pawned.
The women got restless.
The bottles bled dry.

But the poems still come.
They writhe in the belly,
They brag a tragic knowing,
Rising like a sensuous flame
and riding out to you.

My Muse Arrived Around One A.M.

The fine and luxurious,
Such pretty dolls.
I love 'em all.

With feathers and fish-hook smiles,
Adorned and glorious, I guess you'd say.
But there's always something missing,
The groomed steed or seemingly flawless angel
May have a hollow leg
Or a wooden heart,
A headache hatching the future,
Bleeding ulcers, whatever.

And something is always happening around the corner
Or lurking behind grey country eyes.
For in this silly game of poems, money
Existence (?)
There are no head starts or grand finales.
Surely everybody knows that by now.

As the peacock sings
I listen to the walls around me
Rattle and moan
And a midnight wind carries a cloud
Past my window
Like smoke rings wafting through time-bomb air.

Ode To Bar Napkins

Just staring into the neon bar drizzle,
Wondering upon a swizzle stick.

And it's rum and cokes
Dirty jokes
With guitar crash blues
Stirring drunken hearts
Longing for less wisdom than brought on by
The deep retreat of aloneness.

All full of promisary lines
And dancing along a tight-rope of chances.
Wrapped in undertaker make-up.
Clap hands!
And the torch song anthems deafen the night.

Hey, let's get out of here
And go racing rainy streets
Singing a Bukowski song half remembered.